The Essentia

C000301610

RANGE

SECOND

GENERATION

All models 1994-2001

Your marque expert:
James Taylor

VELOCE PUBLISHING
THE PUBLISHER OF FINE AUTOMOTIVE BOOKS

Alfa Romeo Alfasud (Metcalfe)
Alfa Romeo Alfetta: all saloon/sedan models 1972 to 1984 & coupé models 1974 to 1987 (Metcalfe)
Alfa Romeo Giulia GT Coupé (Booker)
Alfa Romeo Giulia Spider (Booker)
Audi TT (Davies)
Audi TT Mk2 2006 to 2014 (Durnan)
Austin-Healey Big Healeys (Trummel)
BMW Boxer Twins (Henshaw)
BMW E30 3 Series 1981 to 1994 (Hosier)
BMW GS (Henshaw)
BMW X5 (Saunders)
BMW Z3 Roadster (Fishwick)
BMW Z4: E85 Roadster and E86 Coupé including M and Alpina 2003 to 2009 (Smitheram)
BSA 350, 441 & 500 Singles (Henshaw)
BSA 500 & 650 Twins (Henshaw)
BSA Bantam (Henshaw)
Choosing, Using & Maintaining Your Electric Bicycle (Henshaw)
Citroën 2CV (Paxton)
Citroën ID & DS (Heilig)
Cobra Replicas (Ayre)
Corvette C2 Sting Ray 1963-1967 (Falconer)
Datsun 240Z 1969 to 1973 (Newlyn)
DeLorean DMC-12 1981 to 1983 (Williams)
Ducati Bevel Twins (Falloon)
Ducati Desmodue Twins (Falloon)
Ducati Desmoquattro Twins – 851, 888, 916, 996, 998, ST4 1988 to 2004 (Falloon)
Fiat 500 & 600 (Bobbitt)
Ford Capri (Paxton)
Ford Escort Mk1 & Mk2 (Williamson)
Ford Model A – All Models 1927 to 1931 (Buckley)
Ford Model T – All models 1909 to 1927 (Barker)
Ford Mustang – First Generation 1964 to 1973 (Cook)
Ford Mustang (Cook)
Ford RS Cosworth Sierra & Escort (Williamson)
Harley-Davidson Big Twins (Henshaw)
Hillman Imp (Morgan)
Hinckley Triumph triples & fours 750, 900, 955, 1000, 1050, 1200 – 1991-2009 (Henshaw)
Honda CBR FireBlade (Henshaw)
Honda CBR600 Hurricane (Henshaw)
Honda SOHC Fours 1969-1984 (Henshaw)
Jaguar E-Type 3.8 & 4.2 litre (Crespin)
Jaguar E-type V12 5.3 litre (Crespin)

Jaguar Mark 1 & 2 (All models including Daimler 2.5-litre V8) 1955 to 1969 (Thorley)
Jaguar New XK 2005-2014 (Thorley)
Jaguar S-Type – 1999 to 2007 (Thorley)
Jaguar X-Type – 2001 to 2009 (Thorley)
Jaguar XJ-S (Crespin)
Jaguar XJ6, XJ8 & XJR (Thorley)
Jaguar XK 120, 140 & 150 (Thorley)
Jaguar XK8 & XKR (1996-2005) (Thorley)
Jaguar/Daimler XJ 1994-2003 (Crespin)
Jaguar/Daimler XJ40 (Crespin)
Jaguar/Daimler XJ6, XJ12 & Sovereign (Crespin)
Kawasaki Z1 & Z900 (Orritt)
Land Rover Discovery Series 1 (1989-1998) (Taylor)
Land Rover Discovery Series 2 (1998-2004) (Taylor)
Land Rover Series I, II & IIA (Thurman)
Land Rover Series III (Thurman)
Lotus Elan, S1 to Sprint and Plus 2 to Plus 2S 130/5 1962 to 1974 (Vale)
Lotus Europa, S1, S2, Twin-cam & Special 1966 to 1975 (Vale)
Lotus Seven replicas & Caterham 7: 1973-2013 (Hawkins)
Mazda MX-5 Miata (Mk1 1989-97 & Mk2 98-2001) (Crook)
Mazda RX-8 (Parish)
Mercedes Benz Pagoda 230SL, 250SL & 280SL roadsters & coupés (Bass)
Mercedes-Benz 190: all 190 models (W201 series) 1982 to 1993 (Parish)
Mercedes-Benz 280-560SL & SLC (Bass)
Mercedes-Benz S-Class: W126 Series 1979 to 1991 (Zoporowski)
Mercedes-Benz SL R129-series 1989 to 2001 (Parish)
Mercedes-Benz SLK (Bass)
Mercedes-Benz W123 (Parish)
Mercedes-Benz W124 – All models 1984-1997 (Zoporowski)
MG Midget & A-H Sprite (Horler)
MG TD, TF & TF1500 (Jones)
MGA 1955-1962 (Crosier)
MGB & MGB GT (Williams)
MGF & MG TF (Hawkins)
Mini (Paxton)
Morris Minor & 1000 (Newell)
Moto Guzzi 2-valve big twins (Falloon)
New Mini (Collins)
Norton Commando (Henshaw)
Peugeot 205 GTI (Blackburn)
Piaggio Scooters – all modern

two-stroke & four-stroke automatic models 1991 to 2016 (Willis)
Porsche 356 (Johnson)
Porsche 911 (964) (Streather)
Porsche 911 (993) (Streather)
Porsche 911 (996) (Streather)
Porsche 911 (997) – Model years 2004 to 2009 (Streather)
Porsche 911 (997) – Second generation models 2009 to 2012 (Streather)
Porsche 911 Carrera 3.2 (Streather)
Porsche 911SC (Streather)
Porsche 924 – All models 1976 to 1988 (Hodgkins)
Porsche 928 (Hemmings)
Porsche 930 Turbo & 911 (930) Turbo (Streather)
Porsche 944 (Higgins)
Porsche 981 Boxster & Cayman (Streather)
Porsche 986 Boxster (Streather)
Porsche 987 Boxster and Cayman 1st generation (2005-2009) (Streather)
Porsche 987 Boxster and Cayman 2nd generation (2009-2012) (Streather)
Range Rover – First Generation models 1970 to 1996 (Taylor)
Rolls-Royce Silver Shadow & Bentley T-Series (Bobbitt)
Royal Enfield Bullet (Henshaw)
Subaru Impreza (Hobbs)
Sunbeam Alpine (Barker)
Triumph 350 & 500 Twins (Henshaw)
Triumph Bonneville (Henshaw)
Triumph Stag (Mort)
Triumph Thunderbird, Trophy & Tiger (Henshaw)
Triumph TR2 & TR3 - All models (including 3A & 3B) 1953 to 1962 (Conners)
Triumph TR4/4A & TR5/250 - All models 1961 to 1968 (Child & Battyll)
Triumph TR6 (Williams)
Triumph TR7 & TR8 (Williams)
Triumph Trident & BSA Rocket III (Rooke)
TVR S-series (Kitchen)
Velocette 350 & 500 Singles 1946 to 1970 (Henshaw)
Vespa Scooters – Classic 2-stroke models 1960-2008 (Paxton)
Volkswagen Bus (Copping)
Volvo 700/900 Series (Beavis)
Volvo P1800/1800S, E & ES 1961 to 1973 (Murray)
VW Beetle (Copping)
VW Golf GTI (Copping)

www.veloce.co.uk

First published in April 2019 by Veloce Publishing Limited, Veloce House, Parkway Farm Business Park, Middle Farm Way, Poundbury, Dorchester DT1 3AR, England. Tel +44 (0)1305 260068 / Fax 01305 250479 / e-mail info@veloce.co.uk / web www.veloce.co.uk or www.velocebooks.com.
ISBN: 978-1-787114-32-6; UPC: 6-36847-01432-2.

Introduction
– the purpose of this book

This book is designed to help you buy a second-generation Range Rover that suits your needs and budget. It doesn't have to be in like-new condition, but it does have to be the best you can find within your budget so that you get the best possible value for money. If you want to treat it as a pampered 'classic,' then that's great news. On the other hand, if you just want to enjoy owning and running it as an everyday vehicle, that's just fine. There's another dimension to ownership, too: these Range Rovers have quite astonishing off-road ability, and in my view it would be a shame to own one and never to find out just how capable it is.

These second-generation models went through a complex development process, originally known as Project Discovery, changing to Project Pegasus when the Discovery name was chosen for a different Land Rover product, and then becoming Project 38A when the Pegasus name leaked out to the press. The motor trade got it wrong at a very early stage and chose to call them P38 models, and as a result most people do the same these days – even at Land Rover. This isn't the place to argue, so in this book I'm sticking to calling them second-generation Range Rovers.

This Range Rover represented a quantum leap forward for Land Rover as a company because it was designed from the start as a luxury model to compete with conventional luxury saloons. Even the original Range Rover had been designed as a more comfortable Land Rover, and had gradually worked its way up to luxury status. So it wasn't surprising that some aspects of the vehicle weren't as they should have been when it was launched. Early examples gained a reputation for problems, and that reputation has stayed with the model ever since, even though better quality control had dealt with most of them by about 1998.

I was lucky enough to be invited to the original press launch at Cliveden in autumn 1994, so I've known these Range Rovers since the beginning. I've also driven very many of them, both on the road and off it, thanks to Land Rover's press department and to a few fellow enthusiasts. All this experience has left me with the firm view that a well-sorted second-generation Range Rover is an enjoyable classic – and that a rogue one is quite the opposite. So this book is here to help you avoid the rogue ones and to enjoy one of these models as they were meant to be enjoyed.

Many of the pictures in this book, by the way, were supplied by Land Rover, or Jaguar Land Rover as they have since become. Many others came from my camera, and there are also several taken by my colleague and friend Nick Dimbleby – to whom, as always, go my grateful thanks.

Contents

1 Is it the right car for you?
– marriage guidance

Tall and short drivers

There's good headroom for tall drivers, and the wide range of seat adjustment means that short drivers can also get comfortable. Some shorter people find that the step up into a Range Rover is a stretch unless it is fitted with side-steps.

Controls

The arrays of switches across the top of the centre console and below the heater control panel were designed to look impressive and high-tech at the time, but can be confusing to a newcomer. Their functions have to be learned. The automatic climate control system is very good.

Second-generation Range Rovers were designed to compete with conventional luxury cars, and were equipped to high standards. This is an early 4.6 HSE.

Some controls were mounted on the steering wheel. This wheel, with its half-wood rim, is on a 2001 model.

The Command Driving Position, which gives an excellent view of the road ahead, is a key characteristic.

Will it fit in the garage?

A second-generation Range Rover is 185.6in (4713mm) long, and 74.4in (1890mm) wide with the mirrors folded. At standard ride height, it stands 71.6in (1817mm) tall. You will probably have to fold in the door mirrors for most domestic garages, because the vehicle is otherwise 87.7in (2228mm) wide.

Interior space

These models were designed to seat four people in great comfort, or five people in rather less for the three rear passengers.

Clear and simple instrumentation is matched by an electronic 'message centre.'

Legroom in the rear is good, even when a tall driver has the seat a long way back.

Luggage capacity

The load area will easily carry holiday luggage for four people. With the rear seat in use, the usable load area is 18.5 cubic feet (0.520 cubic metres). With the rear seat folded, this increases to 58 cubic feet (1.643 cubic metres). The rear seat has a 60/40 split-fold design that increases the versatility of the load area.

Usability
Good acceleration and cruising speeds, plus excellent braking and manoeuvrability, make these Range Rovers perfectly acceptable for everyday use.

Parts availability
Most items to keep the car in running order are readily available. However, some non-mechanical items are becoming difficult to find, and the parts unique to the special editions are in many cases impossible to obtain.

Plus points
It is a comfortable and spacious family vehicle that is also a great tow-car and has excellent off-road ability. Most essential maintenance can be done on a DIY basis, although diagnostic equipment will be needed for many electronic items, such as the ABS.

Minus points
These Range Rovers do not like sitting unused for long periods of time, so it is best not to buy one unless you intend to use it fairly regularly! The vehicles are also prone to rashes of electrical problems – some more than others. Fuel consumption of the V8 models in particular is much higher than on more modern 4x4 vehicles.

With the rear seats folded forward, the load space is positively cavernous.

The spare wheel lives under the boot floor – and is very heavy!

Most early models have two airbags (although some for overseas markets did not). Later ones have additional airbags to protect passengers in side impacts.

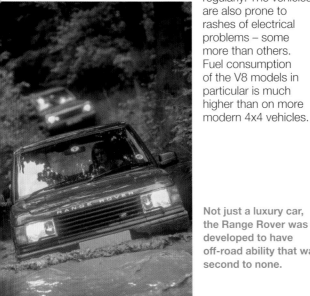

Not just a luxury car, the Range Rover was developed to have off-road ability that was second to none.

2 Cost considerations
– affordable, or a money pit?

Servicing intervals

Land Rover recommended that these Range Rovers should have a main service every 12,000 miles (20,000km) and that diesel-engined models should also have an intermediate one mid-way between each main service. Many owners like to change the oil in a V8 engine every 6000 miles, or even more frequently.

A non-franchised specialist will typically charge around ●x300 for the main service on a V8 model and ●x400 on a diesel model. The cost of additional parts needed, such as new brake pads, filters, and so on, will be extra.

Sample parts prices

Prices can vary considerably, and those shown here are typical. Buying OE items from Land Rover is the most expensive solution. Many pattern parts are available, but not all are made to OE standards. All prices are shown before VAT is added.

Air spring (rear)	●x45
Alternator	●x165 (105 amp type, for diesel)
	●x125 (120 amp type, for V8)
Brake pads	●x75 (front axle set); ●x30 (rear axle set)
Exhaust system	●x200 (diesel, single pipe, stainless steel)
	●x240 (diesel, twin pipe, stainless steel)
	●x200 (V8, single pipe, stainless steel, less catalyst)
	●x650 (V8, single pipe, stainless steel, with catalyst)
Headlamp	●x205 (pre-facelift)
	●x220 upwards (facelift)
Radiator	●x115 (diesel, manual)
	●x125 (diesel, automatic)
	●x90 (V8)
Shock absorber	●x35 upwards, depending on type
Steering damper	●x35 upwards
Tyre	●x55 upwards (16in), depending on type
	●x110 upwards (18in), depending on type
Wiper blade	●x3 (aftermarket)

Parts that are easy to find

Aftermarket suppliers can usually provide all the consumable items needed to keep a Range Rover in running order, although in some cases you may have to compromise on quality. Most mechanical items are available, but it is sometimes necessary to search quite hard for them.

Parts that are hard to find

There are few items that are hard to find, although Land Rover does have periodic shortages of less commonly ordered parts.

Beware!

Neglected examples of the second-generation Range Rover definitely fall into the 'money pit' category. This is not a vehicle than can be run on a shoestring budget.

3 Living with a Range Rover
– will you get along together?

Living with a second-generation Range Rover can be a thoroughly enjoyable experience – or it can be an expensive nightmare. When functioning as Land Rover intended, these are very refined vehicles with a feeling of dependability and strength about them. However, bad examples – and there have been many – reward their owners with a constant stream of minor problems, and sometimes major ones as well. So it is vitally important to read the buying advice that is contained in this book in order to avoid a bad one.

The driving experience is quite special, with a high seating position and an excellent view all round. Despite its size, a Range Rover does not (or should not) feel cumbersome, although simple laws of physics mean that it does not take kindly to being thrown about like a small hatchback. Weight means that it will not accelerate like one, either, despite the size of the engines, although acceleration at motorway speeds is satisfyingly rapid in the V8 models; it is very much less so in the diesels. With both engine types, the

The thirstiest engine of all is the 4.6-litre V8, seen here in an early model. The later 'Thor' engines had a different appearance, with a tubular manifold on top of the engine.

The on-board computer of this early 4.6 HSE calculated the fuel consumption after around 200 miles of mixed driving. There was no reason to argue ...

The BMW diesel engine is a smooth six-cylinder, but not ideal with an automatic gearbox in the Range Rover.

Not all seats were leather, and not all gearboxes were automatic. These are the cloth seats and manual gearshift in an early diesel model.

permanent four-wheel drive provides fuss-free traction and roadholding in the wet, plus the ability to press on through snow if necessary.

At this point, it's worth mentioning one of the basic decisions about ownership on a second-generation Range Rover, and that is whether to choose a diesel engine or one of the V8 petrol engines. We'll come back to this question later in the book, but the two types are like chalk and cheese. The diesels are fine for relaxed driving and are obviously cheaper to run, but many people find their performance disappointing. The full Range Rover experience comes from the V8 petrol engines, and those are thirsty. With a V8, you will struggle to better 18-20mpg on a regular basis, especially with an automatic gearbox, but the diesels can manage 25mpg and better if used gently. Obviously, enjoying the V8's performance too much will cost you at the petrol pumps!

A second decision associated with ownership is whether you intend to make use of the Range Rover's formidable off-road ability. These vehicles were designed with genuine

Top models have a complex set of seat adjustment controls.

Lower-specification models have manual adjustment for the front seats.

all-round capability, and it is perfectly possible to treat one purely as a luxury car or towing vehicle, as many people did when they were new. Equally, it is possible to get immense enjoyment out of using one as a weekend off-roader, when its ability will almost certainly surprise and delight you. Just don't expect to keep the vehicle in pristine 'luxury car' condition if you do a lot of off-roading with it!

At the time of writing, the general public does not perceive a second-generation Range Rover as a classic vehicle. That will probably come later – although it may take some time. So despite their elegance and presence, these Range Rovers are not head-turners. In fact, it's probably true to say that they were designed to be discreet – and they succeeded only too well.

As for looking after a Range Rover, never forget that the sheer size and weight of these vehicles mean that lack of maintenance can soon lead to safety-related problems. So never skimp on servicing; there are many specialists who can do the job for you competently and affordably. However, don't expect every village garage to be able – or even willing – to carry out the more complex jobs. A Range Rover is not your average everyday saloon car, and specialist knowledge does help. The complexity of the electrical systems on these models, and their reputation for being troublesome, may well discourage non-specialist garages from taking on even the simplest of maintenance tasks for you.

There is no reason why you should not look after your Range Rover yourself. Routine servicing is not difficult, as long as you have a decent workshop manual and the appropriate tools. Buy the parts manual for your model, too (there are several different ones, covering different ages of Range Rover). The ones that Land Rover itself produced contain exploded diagrams that are very useful for the DIY mechanic. Probably the best compromise is to do as much as possible of the routine maintenance yourself, but to find a local specialist who will help you out or take on the more difficult jobs for you. Typically, the jobs that DIY maintenance cannot cover are the ones that need specialist diagnostic equipment. So saying, though, several affordable DIY-friendly diagnostic systems are now becoming available.

Still wondering about using it off-road? It was designed to cope, and to cope very well indeed. Take no notice of people who tell you that you'll need chunky tyres and a two-inch suspension lift. They are just not necessary unless you aim to do some really extreme stuff: a Range Rover is that good, straight out of the box.

A useful load space: those are two standard-sized, four-drawer filing cabinets in there.

The basic shape of the second-generation Range Rover did not change between its introduction in 1994 and the end of production in 2001. On the visual side, the 2000 models introduced in autumn 1999 brought 'masked' headlamps, clear lenses for the front indicators and wing-mounted repeaters, and smoked lenses for the tail lights.

There was a quite extensive range of accessories; this Vogue model has optional roof bars and a roof stowage box. Are such things important to you?

The diesel engine was a turbocharged 2.5-litre six-cylinder BMW type (called the M51). The petrol engines were both all-aluminium V8s and came in two sizes – 4.0-litre and 4.6-litre. Early V8s had a Lucas GEMS management system, and the later 'Thor' engines had a Bosch Motronic system; the later V8s have slightly less outright power, but better driveability at higher speeds.

The later alloy wheels were more attractive than the early designs. This is the Hurricane type, with an 18-inch diameter.

There were both manual and automatic gearboxes, although the manual gearbox was never available with the 4.6-litre V8 engine. The manual gearbox is a five-speed type with an overdrive top gear and is called the R380. The automatic is a ZF, type 4HP22 for the diesel and 4.0-litre V8, or the stronger 4HP24 for the 4.6-litre V8.

The entry-level models were the 2.5DT (diesel), 4.0 (petrol), and later County models; typically, they came with cloth upholstery. Next up were the SE and DSE models, with leather upholstery and the automatic climate control system. Above this were the HSE and DHSE types, with generally higher levels of convenience equipment, plus wood trim on the doors. In autumn 1999 came a new top Vogue trim, typically with ruched leather upholstery.

The 4.0-litre V8 is probably the best all-round engine, as long as fuel consumption is not an issue.

The later 'Thor' V8 engines have a tubular manifold and greater flexibility at motorway speeds.

There were also several special editions, with combinations of features not available elsewhere. On top of that, Land Rover ran a custom-finishing scheme called 'Autobiography' that pioneered special features and individual paint and trim combinations.

So which should you buy? It's always best to buy on condition, but if there's a choice, go for the better-equipped models. They offer more features and won't cost significantly more than lower-specification types. Automatic V8s are undoubtedly the nicest to drive, and for that reason are likely to be most expensive. Sellers of special editions often promote their rarity and price them accordingly; most buyers take some persuading to pay more than for a broadly comparable standard model.

It's advisable to have at least an outline knowledge of the model designations. The Vogue 50 was a special edition celebrating 50 years of Land Rover in 1998.

Left: 2.5 DHSE translates as a 2.5-litre diesel with the high-level HSE specification; these were available in the 2000 model-year.

Centre: The late-model Vogue SE had the highest specification available outside the Autobiography scheme.

Right: Later models had 'masked' headlamps and clear front indicators, as seen here.

5 Before you view
– be well informed

To avoid a wasted journey, and the disappointment of finding that the Range Rover does not match your expectations, it will help if you're very clear about what questions you want to ask before you pick up the telephone. Some of these points might appear basic, but when you're excited about the prospect of buying your dream classic, it's amazing how some of the most obvious things slip the mind ... Also check the current values in classic car magazines which give both a price guide and auction results.

Where is the car?
Is it going to be worth travelling to the next county/state, or even across a border? A locally advertised car, although it may not sound very interesting, can add to your knowledge for very little effort, so make a visit – it might even be in better condition than expected.

Dealer or private sale
Establish early on if the car is being sold by its owner or by a trader. A private owner should have all the history, so don't be afraid to ask detailed questions. A dealer may have more limited knowledge of a car's history, but should have some documentation. A dealer may offer a warranty/guarantee (ask for a printed copy) and finance.

Cost of collection and delivery
A dealer may quote for delivery by car transporter. A private owner may agree to meet you halfway, but only agree to this after you have seen the car at the vendor's address to validate the documents. Conversely, you could meet halfway and agree the sale, but insist on meeting at the vendor's address for the handover.

View – when and where?
It is always preferable to view at the vendor's home or business premises. In the case of a private sale, the car's documentation should tally with the vendor's name and address. Arrange to view only in daylight and avoid a wet day. Most cars look better in poor light or when wet.

Reason for sale
Do make it one of the first questions. Why is the car being sold and how long has it been with the current owner? How many previous owners?

Left-hand drive to right-hand drive, and 'specials'
You are most unlikely to find a Range Rover which has been converted from LHD to RHD (or vice versa); the job is too expensive and difficult to be financially viable. However, there were some special high-performance Range Rover conversions – notably by Overfinch and JE Engineering. These have a special interest to hard-core enthusiasts but are likely to need special maintenance as well.

Condition (body/chassis/interior/mechanicals)
Ask for an honest appraisal of the car's condition. Ask specifically about some of the check items described in chapter 7.

All original specification

An original equipment car is invariably of higher value than a customised version.

Matching data/legal ownership

Do VIN/chassis, engine numbers and license plate match the official registration document? Is the owner's name and address recorded in the official registration documents?

For those countries that require an annual test of roadworthiness, does the car have a document showing it complies (an MoT certificate in the UK, which can be verified on 0845 600 5977)? If a smog/emissions certificate is mandatory, does the car have one? If required, does the car carry a current road fund licence/licence plate tag? Does the vendor own the car outright? Money might be owed to a finance company or bank: the car could even be stolen.

Several organisations will supply the data on ownership, based on the car's licence plate number, for a fee. Such companies can often also tell you whether the car has been 'written off' by an insurance company. In the UK these organisations can supply vehicle data:

HPI – 01722 422 422
AA – 0870 600 0836
DVLA – 0870 240 0010
RAC – 0870 533 3660

Other countries will have similar organisations.

Unleaded fuel

All petrol-engined second-generation Range Rovers were designed to run on unleaded fuel and came with catalytic converters as standard.

Insurance

Check with your existing insurer before setting out; your current policy might not cover you to drive the car if you do purchase it.

How you can pay

A cheque/check will take several days to clear and the seller may prefer to sell to a cash buyer. However, a banker's draft (a cheque issued by a bank) is as good as cash, but safer, so contact your own bank and become familiar with the formalities that are necessary to obtain one.

Buying at auction?

If the intention is to buy at auction, see chapter 10 for further advice.

Professional vehicle check (mechanical examination)

There are often marque/model specialists who will undertake professional examination of a vehicle on your behalf. Owners' clubs will be able to put you in touch with such specialists.

Other organisations that will carry out a general professional check in the UK are:
AA – 0800 085 3007 (motoring organisation with vehicle inspectors)
ABS – 0800 358 5855 (specialist vehicle inspection company)
RAC – 0870 533 3660 (motoring organisation with vehicle inspectors)
Other countries will have similar organisations.

6 Inspection equipment
– these items will really help

This book
Reading glasses (if you need them for close work)
Magnet (not powerful, a fridge magnet is ideal)
Torch
Probe (a small screwdriver works very well)
Overalls
Mirror on a stick
Digital camera
A friend, preferably a knowledgeable enthusiast

Before you rush out of the door, gather together a few items that will help as you work your way around the Range Rover. This book is designed to be your guide at every step, so take it along and use the check boxes to help you assess each area of the car you're interested in. Don't be afraid to let the seller see you using it. Take your reading glasses if you need them to read documents and make close up inspections.

A magnet will help you check if the car is full of filler, or has fibreglass panels. Use the magnet to sample bodywork areas all around the car, but be careful not to damage the paintwork. Expect to find a little filler here and there, but not whole panels. There's nothing wrong with fibreglass panels, but a purist might want the vehicle to be as original as possible.

A torch with fresh batteries will be useful for peering into the wheelarches and under the vehicle.

A small screwdriver can be used – with care – as a probe, particularly in the wheelarches and on the underside. With this you should be able to check an area of severe corrosion, but be careful – if it's really bad the screwdriver might go right through the metal!

Be prepared to get dirty. Take along a pair of overalls, if you have them. Fixing a mirror at an angle on the end of a stick may seem odd, but you'll probably need it to check the condition of the underside of the vehicle. It will also help you to peer into some of the important crevices. You can also use it, together with the torch, along the underside of the sills and on the floor.

If you have the use of a digital camera, take it along so that later you can study some areas of the car more closely. Take a picture of any part of the car that causes you concern, and seek a second opinion.

Ideally, have a friend or knowledgeable enthusiast accompany you: a second opinion is always valuable.

7 Fifteen minute evaluation
– walk away or stay?

Before you set off to look at a second-generation Range Rover, make sure you know what variety to expect. It may have a 4.0-litre V8 engine, but is the gearbox manual or automatic? What is the trim and equipment level? You can find out more about what to expect from some of the books listed on page 57.

You can often get a good idea of what to expect of the vehicle itself from the place where you go to look at it. Rough area? Farmyard? Backstreet dealer? Neat suburban drive? The location can tell you things about a Range Rover that the seller won't mention. Form your own opinion.

It's very easy to make one of these Range Rovers look newer than it really is to an inexperienced eye – all that's necessary is a set of face-lift-specification (2000 model-year) lights and some new alloy wheels: make sure that you are not being conned! Seat styles are a good guide: owners very rarely change the early seats to the later type. Of course, you may not object to these cosmetic changes at all if they make the vehicle more like what you want. On the other hand, they may well make it valueless to somebody who wants one in original condition.

The condition of the four corners gives a good clue to how well the vehicle has been looked after. Scrapes will be very noticeable on the later painted bumper aprons.

Exterior

It's logical to start with a look at the outside of the Range Rover, and certain things should be very obvious from the beginning. The state of the paintwork is the first one: dull paintwork immediately suggests that a vehicle has not been maintained to a high standard. Equally, glossy paintwork may simply indicate that the vendor has been busy with the polish just prior to your arrival! However, other clues are harder to cover up. Check the condition of the bumpers and aprons, especially at the four corners of the vehicle. Misalignment and scrapes will tell their own story.

Air suspension will sink over time – and this one certainly has: the vehicle had actually been standing for several months when photographed, and the tyre had lost air as well.

It will be very obvious whether the vehicle sits all-square and at the correct ride height. If not, suspect problems with the air suspension; this may be no more than a leaking air spring (which is not expensive to replace), but there could also be a much more expensive fault. Now take a look at the wheels and tyres. All these Range Rovers came with alloy wheels when they were new, and those alloy wheels can get damaged. The 16-inch size is usually well protected by the deeper sidewalls of the tyres, but the 18-inch wheels are often damaged on kerbs. Obviously, it's a good idea to check the tread on all the tyres as well. Signs of uneven wear are more worrying than tyres that are simply worn with use; make sure that you check the spare tyre as well, because a little-worn spare may have been put on to hide the uneven wear on another tyre!

Now have a good look round the body, hunting for any signs of accident repair. Quality accident repairs are fine, and usually invisible; it's the cheap ones that you're looking for. Poor-quality repairs will be apparent in uneven door and bonnet gaps; panel gaps were something that Land Rover did get right on the second-generation Range Rover, even though its predecessor was well known for having large and inconsistent gaps. Poor-quality repairs can also be betrayed by rust in the panels, because rust is not normally a problem on these models.

Two other things may have become apparent during this walk-round. One is whether the Range Rover has been used for towing. There's no real problem if it has, but it's worth making some gentle enquiries about what it has towed. Regular towing of heavily-laden trailers will certainly have accelerated wear in the driveline, for example. If it's a V8 model, the second thing that will be apparent is whether it's been fitted with an LPG conversion: the filler cap is usually located just behind the right-hand rear wheel in the lower body valance. Again, there's no problem with this in principle, but do make sure that an LPGA certificate is available to confirm that the installation meets all the applicable standards. Without one, you may have trouble getting the vehicle insured.

On the inside

Now look inside the passenger cabin. The condition of the upholstery will be immediately

Missing or damaged letters on bonnet and tailgate are very definitely not a sign of a well-kept Range Rover. Note, too, how the grey plastic grille has lightened in colour thanks to sunlight and lack of cleaning.

Not good signs! The paint is dull and there are signs of neglect in the green mould and damage to the black window frames, while the chip out of the tail-light lens tells its own story.

This was the factory-approved tow hitch, although it was by no means the only type ever fitted. If the Range Rover has a towbar, what sort of towing has it been doing?

The message centre comes up with some surprisingly obvious messages; it's when no messages come up that there are problems.

The wear on this driver's seat is immediately obvious, and the missing cover on the seat belt receiver is another indication of how the vehicle has been used.

apparent, and while a few creases in the leather (especially on the driver's seat) are the honourable scars of use, torn or stained leather is something you don't want to see. If there's a dog guard behind the rear seat, check for signs of damage caused by a hyperactive pooch in the load bay. It's also worth checking for signs of dog damage on the back seat and door trims, even if no dog guard is fitted!

Take a good look in the front footwells and, if overmats have been fitted, lift them up to look underneath. Wet carpets are a bad sign, and usually mean that there is a leak from the heater unit. It can be fixed, even as a DIY job, but it's awkward and time-consuming. Check that the ICE head unit is the original one and, if it is, ask the owner if the original radio anti-theft code is available. Without it, the head unit won't work. The code is likely to be written down somewhere in the vehicle literature, along with the immobiliser code that you will also need in case of problems.

Ask if you can start the vehicle. Once you've turned the key, make sure that all the warning lights come on and then extinguish after their self-checking procedure, which takes about eight seconds. If it's the first time you've fired up one of these Range Rovers, you won't necessarily know what to look for, but don't worry – you can make a more detailed check when and if you come back for a second look. Now start the engine. The ABS warning light should remain on, and will not go out until the Range Rover has exceeded 5mph, so you will need to drive the vehicle for a short distance to check this.

Something else to look out for at this stage is reluctant starting. Is the engine cold, or has it been warmed up for you to hide a problem? On a V8-engined car, a slow starter cranking speed is probably caused by a weak battery; remember that some people will buy a smaller battery than is really needed in order to save money. On a diesel, poor starting from cold suggests that the glow plugs are not doing their job properly, or perhaps that the fuel lift pump is worn.

Second-generation Range Rovers are notorious for developing annoying problems, and typically electrical ones. Now is not the time for a thorough check, which you can save until you come back for a second look at the vehicle, but it might be worth making sure that the electric windows all work, that the driver's seat electric adjustment is functional (lower-spec models have manual adjustment), and that the sunroof operates if one is fitted.

This is the engine bay of a well-used 4.0-litre V8 model. The corrosion on the body of the alternator is quite normal, although it can be cleaned up. Brake and coolant levels seem okay – but what is that bundle of black insulation tape on the battery cable? The battery, incidentally, is normally hidden under a plastic cover.

Under the bonnet

Everybody likes to take a look under the bonnet. The bonnet release is on the outboard side of the driver's footwell, and should release the bonnet onto its safety catch. The safety catch is under the centre of the bonnet, above the radiator grille, and

The 18-inch wheels certainly look good, and this is the Hurricane type available on later models. However, the shallower tyre sidewalls with these larger wheels make the wheels more vulnerable to kerbing damage.

you release it by pressing on a small platform that's provided for the purpose. The bonnet will then rise automatically on gas struts – or at least it will unless these struts are worn. Once you've seen what you want to in the engine bay, lift the bonnet slightly to disengage the locking strut, gently lower the bonnet until it's about a foot above the locking platform, and then push it down with the palms of both hands until the catches engage.

Mostly, what you'll be looking for under the bonnet are signs of leaks, predominantly of oil and coolant, although a generally unkempt appearance should also ring alarm bells. Look especially for signs of coolant leaking down the sides of the cylinder block from the joint(s) with the cylinder head(s) – the diesel engine is particularly prone to head gasket troubles, but the V8s are certainly not immune to them. Water loss from a V8 might also be caused by the so-called 'porous block' problem, which is actually caused by the cylinder liners coming loose in the block and is expensive to rectify. With the engine switched off, make sure that you feel the radiator hoses on V8s: rock-hard hoses mean that the cooling system has become pressurised, and this is a symptom of the 'porous block' condition.

Underneath

Don't forget to have at least a quick look underneath the vehicle. You can save a detailed inspection until later – if you go back for a second look at this particular vehicle – but now is the time to check for those suspicious-looking oil stains on the ground.

The good news is that the chassis frames of these Range Rovers have not shown any particular tendency to rust. In fact, their rust resistance seems to be higher than that of many other separate-chassis Land Rover products. So very visible rust is something out of the ordinary and will merit further investigation right away. It's also not unknown for the chassis frame to sustain some damage in severe off-road use, and your quick inspection at this stage should enable you to spot any major horrors.

Lastly, take a look at the springs to make sure they really are the original black rubber air springs. Recurrent problems with the air suspension on some vehicles prompted a few owners to swap the air springs for a set of steel coil springs as used on the earlier Range Rover. As long as all the other air suspension hardware has been disabled, this isn't likely to be a particular problem. However, the ride quality with coil springs is not as good as that with the original air suspension and, if it matters to you, the vehicle's originality has also been compromised.

Special editions

It's beyond the scope of this book to go into the minutiae of the special-edition Range Rovers. You'll need to take an expert along for that, or at least be very certain of what you expect to find before you go to view a vehicle. However, a couple of points are worth bearing in mind. One is that Land Rover often created special editions by adding accessories to otherwise standard models, so making them look like good value for money. They are therefore not all laden with exotic options. The other is that

The acid test: how does it drive on the road?

You should never see this, and the picture is here just to satisfy your curiosity about airbags. This is how the passenger's side airbag is stowed behind the dashboard – all neatly folded.

buyers generally assess special editions on their overall level of equipment rather than on their rarity; don't be tempted to pay over the odds.

Autobiography models are another special category. Most were individually specified by their first owners, although there was also an Autobiography limited edition. Beware of unique features for which replacement parts are not available (some of the video systems fall into this category), and be prepared to accept the quirky taste of the person who ordered the car when it was new.

A sagging headlining is a fairly common problem. Don't imagine that you will be able to repair it; budget for a replacement.

Leaks from the sunroof drain tubes can cause headlining problems and dampness elsewhere. This demonstration cutaway model shows the drain tube on the left of the car, leading from the front edge of the sunroof cassette. All this is normally concealed by the headlining.

How does it go/sound/feel?

The last element of this 15-minute initial evaluation is likely to be a short test drive. Don't forget that you will need to be insured to drive the vehicle and that not every insurance policy covers you for using somebody else's vehicle. Also worth checking is that the vehicle itself is road legal; if you take a test drive on a public road in a vehicle without a valid roadworthiness certificate, you will be breaking the law.

The BMW diesel engine has an unmistakable, if subdued, diesel rattle at idle, but makes quite business-like noises while accelerating. Turbocharger boost should be undetectable as it cuts in, and there should be no sudden transition; check in the rear window for black smoke when accelerating, which could be either from wear in the injection system or a turbocharger problem. If this is the first time you have driven a second-generation Range Rover with a diesel engine, it may also be the point at which you realise these vehicles are rather under-powered, at least with an automatic gearbox. 'Chips' have been available to increase the torque, and are generally a worthwhile investment; ask if one has been fitted.

Any V8 engine should always pull cleanly and smoothly, although high-mileage or neglected examples may have some top-end clatter from worn valve-gear. Keep an eye on the dashboard instruments for signs of overheating, which is always unwelcome in an all-aluminium engine. Listen, too, for the characteristic sound at idle of exhaust gases leaking through a manifold that needs to be tightened up. The remedy is straightforward, but a leak may prove a bargaining point later on.

Does the Range Rover run in a straight line if you take your hands off the wheel? Only do this very briefly, of course. Does it pull up in a straight line when you brake? There should not be any driveline shunt, and there should be no more than a gentle movement on automatic models as drive or reverse is engaged from neutral; if there is a heavy thump or a bang in the driveline, something is amiss. Automatic changes should be smooth both up and down the gearbox, and if they aren't, there's a problem. Slurring on upchanges indicates wear.

With a manual gearbox, listen for gears that chatter on the over-run, and make sure that all gears can be selected, including reverse. Check that second and third do not jump out of engagement on the over-run. Don't forget that the transfer box lever can seize up if unused for long periods. So select low ratio, and make sure it engages; there's a dashboard button on manual models, and on automatics you access low range through the H-gate selector. Both types have a servo motor to engage low range, and the motor can seize through lack of use. There is no separate control for the centre differential lock, which is actuated automatically by a viscous coupling.

Paperwork

Lastly, take a look at the paperwork. Is the seller's name on the documentation? Do the chassis and engine numbers match those on the vehicle? How long has the seller owned it? Problem vehicles are often sold on very quickly.

If the vehicle has been modified significantly, check that these modifications have the approval of the local authorities. In some countries, what you can do to a vehicle (for example, to improve its off-road ability) is limited by legislation.

8 Key points
– where to look for problems

After your preliminary look at the Range Rover you're thinking of buying, you'll want to spend some time thinking over what you've seen and deciding whether to go for a second look – which is what the next chapter is all about.

In the meantime, though, you'll need to sort out the potentially confusing mass of information that you've just gathered so that you can make some sense of it. So, begin by focussing on some key points:
• Is the vehicle structurally sound?
• Is it cosmetically acceptable?
• Does the engine seem good?

If the answers to these questions are all 'Yes,' you're probably going to want to go back for another, more detailed look. If there are any 'No' answers there, the chances are that you'll decide to give this one a miss.

If you're still thinking you might buy that vehicle, here are a couple more deal-breaker questions:
• How much work will you have to do to it to make it meet your standards?
• Is it really the Range Rover you want? For example, does it have cloth seats when you really wanted leather?
• Are you going to have to do some tricky explaining to your wife/husband/significant other when you get it home?

If you've been honest in your answers to these questions, and you still think you might buy the vehicle, move on to the next chapter.

Previous owners may well have adapted the Range Rover to suit their own tastes, and the profusion of extra lights on this one may not be what you had in mind. Yes, the lights and that nudge bar can be removed – but will you be left with unsightly mounting holes to fill?

Are you quite sure this is the one you want? Diesel and petrol V8 models have very different driving characteristics, and for most people are not simply interchangeable choices.

Special editions may be quite tempting, as long as all the special features remain undamaged or functional, but the 'centre-fill' speaker on the dashboard of the Westminster model was no thing of beauty.

If you really wanted a satnav system but the vehicle doesn't have it, think carefully whether this is the right one for you.

9 Serious evaluation

– 60 minutes for years of enjoyment

Score each section using the boxes as follows: 4 = Excellent; 3 = Good; 2 = Average; 1 = Poor. The totting-up procedure is explained at the end of the chapter. Be realistic in your marking!

The best way to use this section is to tick the boxes as you go along, because you won't be able to remember all the details of the vehicle when you sit down to think about it later on. The inspection sequence follows a logical order, so you'll start with the outside of the vehicle, move on to the interior, then examine the engine bay and the underside. Last of all, you'll take a test drive.

Paintwork

Over the years, three types of paint were available on the second-generation Range Rover. These were 'solid' types, metallic types, and micatallic types. Most of these are 'c-o-b' or clear-over-base types, with a clear protective varnish as standard. Check for signs of touching-in and repainting. It is not easy to get a good paint match for the metallic colours by doing a partial respray of a panel, and it will usually be very obvious if this has been done. Use it as a bargaining point if it has.

Metallic paints are the most difficult to touch in, and new paint almost invariably shows. This is a special metallic green Autobiography model.

The paint finish on the second-generation Range Rover was always very good, so be suspicious of areas where the paintwork seems to fall below standard. Typically, these will be areas that have been repainted, and you need to find out why the repainting had to be done. Was the vehicle involved in a collision? If so, this should alert you to look for other signs of damage that may be less visible. Expect to find a few stone chips on the leading edge of the bonnet and, as you'll have spotted in your preliminary evaluation, a few minor scrapes on the corners of the front bumper, and maybe the rear one as well. Not all bumpers were painted: on early models they had a dark grey textured plastic finish.

Body panels

Panel fit on the second-generation Range Rover was very much better than it had traditionally been from Land Rover, so treat any signs of misaligned or poor-fitting panels with suspicion. It means

Less immediately obvious than flaws in the paint are problems with the window frame finish. This whitening is fairly typical.

that something has been replaced, and you need to discover why.

The good news is that these models rarely suffer from panel corrosion problems. So if you spot some, try to find out why it has occurred because it may indicate poor repairs after an accident.

Front wings/fenders   [4] [3] [2] [1]

The front wings on these models are made from aluminium alloy and will therefore not rust. However, it is wise to check the area where the wing panel meets the plastic bumper, as mud and debris trapped here can eventually cause problems. If headlamp guards have been fitted, it is possible for electrolytic reaction between steel screws and the alloy panel to break out around their fixing holes. Removal of the fixing screws can also often lead to panel distortion around the drilled holes.

Accessory lamp guards usually leave holes in the bodywork when removed.

Bonnet   [4] [3] [2] [1]

The bonnet panel is made of steel that is zinc-coated on both sides. It is unlikely to corrode, but stone chip damage can occur around the 'Range Rover' letters on the nose. If these chips have been touched in, the owner has tried to take care of the vehicle; if not, suspect the opposite. The bonnet should be a first-class fit, and any uneven gaps between its edges and the front wings will suggest there has been accident damage and consequent panel replacement.

This cutaway demonstration model shows the construction of the bonnet. The frame rarely rusts, and the skin is zinc-coated.

Doors and tailgate   [4] [3] [2] [1]

The doors and lower tailgate are panelled in aluminium alloy, but the frames are made of steel that has been zinc-coated on each side. They should be an excellent fit. If there are noticeable gaps between a door panel and its rubber bump-strip, that

The cutaway model here shows the arrangement of the door locks, and the side-impact bars inside the doors.

The door handles should pull out smoothly to open the door. Roughness or jamming indicates a problem.

bump-strip has probably been replaced and the door panel beneath may have been distorted.

Make sure the central locking locks and unlocks *all* the doors and the tailgate, as problems are quite common. This may be caused by nothing more than a spring, although replacement is a fiddly job, and it is often wiser to replace the complete lock as a long-term measure.

Roof panel & sunroof 4 3 2 1
(if fitted)

The roof panel is made of coated steel and will not normally have any problems. However, many owners never look at or clean the roof of a Range Rover from the time they buy it; the first sign of neglect is when the clear varnish over the paint starts to peel off. More serious damage may be caused during fitting or removal of a roof rack.

Top models have an electrically operated sunroof. As a first check, make sure that the roof will actually open and close properly. Sunroofs can seize through lack of use, and the electric motor can burn out if the roof itself has seized. Sunroofs can also develop leaks, although this has not yet become a major problem. The main sources of sunroof leaks are the seals, the drain channels, and the pipes that run down inside the windscreen pillars.

Sills/rockers, side-steps 4 3 2 1

Tough plastic side sills run under the doors, and any signs of damage to these sills is worth investigating, because they are rarely damaged, even in off-road use. However, corrosion of the metal body panel behind has shown up on some older examples, and most notably at the rear of the outer sill on the right-hand side. This will require immediate attention if the corrosion is not to spread.

A lot of these Range Rovers were fitted with side-steps, to help smaller people get into a tall vehicle, or with

This is the cutaway model again, showing how the outer door skins are wrapped over the door inner frames.

Always check the state of the roof panel! This Range Rover had clearly spent some time in the open when photographed.

The roof rack was designed to fit into apertures in the roof. Nevertheless, mounting and removing it may cause damage to the roof panel.

This alternative roof rack required only the cross-bars to be removed; the side frames remained in place. Roof damage is less likely with this type.

Land Rover's own side-steps were both stylish and practical – but beware of damaged examples, in case replacements cannot be found.

The battery has its own plastic cover in the engine bay, and that cover should be present.

side runners, to protect the sills. Both are bolted to the chassis, and both are vulnerable to damage. It takes a pretty hard knock to bend such large and solid pieces of metal, so look for other damage that was caused at the same time. If a step or side runner is damaged on one side, remember that finding a matching replacement could be difficult. You might need to replace the steps or runners as a pair.

The engine bay

The Range Rover's engine bay is very well filled, to such an extent that it is quite difficult to get a good look at the bulkhead, the inner wings and the wheelarches. All these panels are made of zinc-coated steel and the wheelarches are protected underneath by liners, but it is advisable to look for signs of debris building up where each wheelarch panel meets the vertical inner wing, and also where it meets the bulkhead. This debris will hold water against the panels and, if the protective coating has been damaged, can lead to rusting. As in other areas that are usually trouble-free, signs of corrosion in either area may be the result of accident damage that has been poorly repaired.

There is a large plastic cover panel on the left of the engine bay as you stand looking into it, which conceals the battery. Undo the securing turnbuckle and lift this cover to take a look. Check for corrosion around the battery terminals (sometimes caused by them being less than fully tight), and check that the battery is of the correct rating: diesel models should have a battery with a minimum 107 amp-hour rating, and the minimum for the V8 petrol models is a 72 amp-hour rating.

Many owners fit larger-capacity batteries because battery drain can be a problem on Range Rovers that are left unused for several days at a time. Ask when the battery was last changed, and bear in mind that a weak battery can be the cause of multiple malfunctions and fault warnings on the dashboard message centre.

Before going on to look at the engine itself, take a moment to check fluid levels. Oil is easily checked by the dipstick; coolant is easily checked by a look at the transparent header tank; and the power

An LPGA sticker on the windscreen is an indication that an LPG system is fitted. The question now is, how well has it been done?

steering reservoir has its own dipstick embedded in the screw cap. Double-check the coolant by looking for signs of leakage on and from the radiator.

Most Range Rovers will still have their original or original type of engine, not least because of the complications associated with changing to another type: the engine has to be 'plumbed in' to various electrical control units whose software is designed only to suit the original type. However, it is quite common to find that both petrol and diesel engines have been tuned for greater power, typically by means of a replacement or 'piggy-back' ECU chip. Several aftermarket specialists have offered these, and a chip-tuned engine should not normally be a cause for concern, but if a chipped engine does prove troublesome, it is worth checking that the chip's electrical connections are intact and have not corroded.

During your preliminary evaluation, you formed an opinion of how well the engine has been maintained. So the next thing is to listen to it running.

The BMW diesel was always noted for its refinement, although it is rather noisier than many modern diesels. It should idle smoothly, so look out for roughness or odd noises. Engines that have been used hard, neglected, or tuned to within an inch of their lives are likely to develop cylinder head problems, so double-check for signs of coolant leaks. These engines have an overheat protection system, activated by a sensor in the cooling system, and this reduces power by limiting the amount of fuel that is injected. An under-performing engine might be suffering from related problems.

The petrol V8s are also quiet and smooth. If there is a lot of top-end noise, there is probably wear in the hydraulic tappets and maybe the camshaft as well, and in anything other than a high-mileage engine this means that oil changes have been neglected. If an LPG conversion has been fitted (see below), there will be a fuel changeover unit that allows the engine to be run on either petrol or on LPG.

Generally, the quieter and smoother a V8 engine sounds, the better its likely condition. These engines need clean oil every 6000 miles, so for peace of mind, ask the owner when the oil was last changed, and confirm that yourself by checking its colour on the dipstick. Black oil indicates an oil change is overdue, and signs of thick black sludge around the oil filler cap mean that maintenance has been neglected in the longer term.

Checking under the car
During your preliminary evaluation, you looked underneath the vehicle. Now have a second look, being a little more thorough in case you missed something the first time – which, in all honesty, is very easy to do.

Spread out a blanket or similar on the ground under the vehicle, and get under there to take a look. Better yet, if you're examining the vehicle in a garage, ask to put the vehicle up on a hoist. Or, if the seller has an inspection pit, ask if the vehicle can be driven over that pit and you can inspect it from underneath. But be warned: many pits collect water, so you may find yourself wading!

Oil and fluid leaks   4 3 2 1
If the Range Rover is leaking oil or other fluids, the evidence will be obvious when you get underneath. Check where the leak is coming from. The more obvious leaks may be of engine oil, and this will typically come from the sump. Oil leaks may also come from axle drain plugs that are not sealing properly, but check also for cracked differential or axle casings, especially on a Range Rover that has been used a lot

This is the cutaway again: the chassis is shown in red, and you can see how it tapers inwards over the front wheels. Also clear is the position of one of the catalytic converters for the V8 engine.

The rear of the chassis is seen in relation to other components. It is much clearer to see in this picture than it ever will be from underneath, with everything in black!

off-road. That sort of damage is going to be expensive to put right.

Note that major fluid leaks from the power steering system, whether from the hydraulic pipes or from the steering box, will lead to refusal of a roadworthiness certificate. Hydraulic pipes are relatively easy and cheap to replace, but a cracked steering box (fortunately quite rare) is not.

Chassis frame

Rust in the chassis frame is not a major problem on these models, and you will have already checked for this and signs of damage earlier. Take another look now, just to be sure, and check in particular for signs of rippling in the chassis members that might have been caused by a collision.

Air suspension

These cars were built with air suspension on all four wheels, and you should begin by checking the condition of each of the air springs. First, check the base of

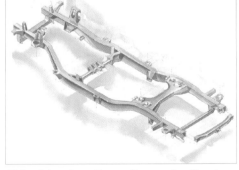

This picture from Range Rover sales literature gives a clear picture of the whole of the chassis frame and its crossmembers.

each rubber air spring, where it meets the axle casing. These springs flex quite a lot in normal use, and eventually the rubber begins to split. With a little more wear, the split becomes an air leak.

Air springs can carry on for quite some time without giving any warning of a problem, because small leaks often seal themselves as the rubber settles differently. However, once a leak becomes more serious, it leads to problems. First – and very obviously – the vehicle may 'collapse' on the side where the spring is

This sketch shows the location of a front air spring and damper (the wheel has been removed for this illustration) ...

... and this shows what an air spring looks like close up. The colours in this picture are created by lighting; in reality, most items will be black except for the brake caliper and disc.

leaking, typically when left parked overnight. Normal height will be restored on start-up in the morning, so that a vehicle can continue in use for a time in this condition. However, remember that the air springs are kept under pressure by the air compressor located in the engine bay, which runs only when the pressure drops below a set level. If the pressure drops regularly, the compressor will be triggered to run more frequently and for longer periods, and eventually it will exceed its design limits and burn out. A replacement air compressor is expensive.

When checking the air suspension system, it is as well to check the condition of the height sensors, which are vertical rods (about as fat as a pencil) mounted to the radius arms at the bottom and pivoting on an arm at the top. These are the triggers for the compressor; if the horizontal arm moves beyond a set level because that corner of the vehicle is sitting low, the compressor is switched on and will pump the springs up. Obviously, any damage here will interfere with the correct working of the height-control system. An internal failure of the sensor can sometimes occur, and there is no known way of predicting this!

Front and rear axles

The axle casings may show signs of off-road damage, typically around the differential housings because these hang lower than the rest of the casing. Severe damage is likely to lead to leaks from the differential, although these will be easy to spot.

At each end of the front axle is a U-shaped section, on which the front wheels swivel when steering. There is also a rubber boot at the end of the drive shaft, and this covers the CV joint that takes drive to the wheel while allowing the wheel to swivel for steering at the same time. The gaiters are commonly split or torn, and this allows road dirt to get into the CV joints and accelerate wear. There should be no oil leaks from the gaiters.

On the rear axle, check the security of the brake pipes that run along its casing. They will probably be held in place by plastic ties, but that is quite good enough to keep them out of harm's way.

The Range Rover has long-travel suspension to give a compliant ride, and cornering roll is tamed by an anti-roll bar on the front axle, although there is no corresponding anti-roll bar at the rear. Check for worn rubber mounting bushes on the anti-roll bar by grasping the bar firmly and trying to move it back and forth. There are also several rubber bushes on the radius arms for both front and rear axles, and there should be no discernible play in these. Worn bushes will in any case become apparent during a test drive, when the vehicle will feel woolly and may wander on the road.

Fuel tank, and LPG conversions

All these Range Rovers have a plastic fuel tank mounted at the rear of the chassis which does not normally give trouble. However, it's wise to check the security of its fixings and for any signs of impact damage to the steel protection plate underneath. This kind of damage can occur in off-road use.

The cost of running a V8-engined Range Rover as an everyday vehicle has persuaded some owners to go for an LPG conversion. LPG has been subject to lower taxation than petrol and, although it is slightly less energy-efficient, it can therefore considerably reduce fuel costs.

An LPG conversion will normally include an extra fuel tank, often fitted under the right-hand side of the body behind the rear wheel. However, some less reputable converters took the easy way out and fitted an extra tank in the load bay, where it obviously reduces load capacity, or in the spare wheel well (which means that the spare has to be carried somewhere else). A Range Rover converted to run on LPG normally retains the ability to run on petrol from the standard fuel tank as well. If an LPG system has been fitted, ask to see evidence that the system has been checked and approved as safe by an appropriate authority if you didn't do so during your earlier inspection. Your insurers may well ask for an engineer's report, too.

Brakes

These Range Rovers have disc brakes on all four wheels, the front pair being ventilated. Check that the correct discs are fitted and that they are not scored or rusty; rust works its way inwards from the outboard edge of a disc. Aftermarket cross-drilled discs have been made available and do a good job as replacements, but the standard brakes give superb stopping power when in good order and there is normally no good reason for fitting an upgraded system.

The handbrake operates on a drum directly behind the transfer gearbox. It locks movement of the rear propshaft, but of course cannot compensate for any movement in the propshaft's universal joints. This accounts for the slight lurch that often occurs on a slope before the handbrake engages – a feature which many people find worrying. It is not unknown for the transmission brake itself to be damaged by a severe impact in off-road driving, but this sort of damage will be obvious.

Steering

Power-assisted steering was standard on all these Range Rovers. Leaks do occur, and you will have checked for obvious ones when looking underneath the vehicle. The PAS fluid used in these vehicles is the familiar red fluid used in many other vehicles, and the second-generation Range Rover does not need the special cold-climate type that is recommended for later Land Rover products – and is very expensive.

The system should not moan or hiss, although the mechanical parts of it may

The PAS fluid reservoir is always at the front of the engine bay, regardless of the engine fitted. This is actually the BMW diesel.

make protesting noises if the wheels are turned on a hard surface while the vehicle is stationary (as often happens in parking manoeuvres). If they do so in other circumstances, there is a problem.

To test for steering problems, you need to have an assistant. Ask the assistant to turn the steering wheel from lock to lock while you get under the vehicle and check for fluid leaks from the PAS box and for movement in the steering linkages. There should be no movement at all between the swivel pin housing and the swivel steering lever at the point where they are bolted together. Free movement in any of the steering assembly's ball joints points to wear.

There is of course also a steering damper, which runs horizontally ahead of the front axle. If there are problems here, your road test later will reveal excessive vibration through the steering wheel.

This sketch shows the layout of the steering components on a left-hand-drive model. The fluid reservoir can be seen in the background; the steering damper is ahead of the steering column; and the anti-roll bar runs across behind the axle and nearest the viewer.

Dampers ④ ③ ② ①

It is difficult to test the dampers (shock absorbers) on a Range Rover by the sort of bounce test that people commonly use for cars. So unless there are obvious fluid leaks from the dampers, or damage to their casings, wait until you drive the vehicle to assess their condition.

Propshafts ④ ③ ② ①

Check for wear in the transmission by grasping the front and rear propshafts in turn and trying to twist them. They will turn slightly as slack in the system is taken up, but if either will rotate as much as a quarter of a turn, there is excessive

Propshafts: both are painted red in this picture of the demonstration cutaway, and the UJs where play can develop are clearly visible. There is of course a UJ at the other end of each propshaft as well.

wear. This may well be in the appropriate differential. When testing the rear propshaft, make sure that the handbrake is off in order not to get a false impression.

While looking at the transmission, check for wear in the universal joints on the propshaft ends by using a screwdriver as a lever to see if there is appreciable movement between the yoke and the joint. The more movement there is, the more advanced that wear will be.

Exhaust system

The standard exhaust systems on these Range Rovers are quite long-lived, especially those on the diesel models. A stainless steel system is a bonus, as it means you are unlikely ever to need a new exhaust. However, do ask to see evidence, such as an invoice, that the system really is stainless steel. It's also as well to check all the mountings, both rigid and flexible.

All petrol-engined Range Rovers have (or should have) catalytic converters in the exhaust system. These 'cats' are very expensive to replace and owners often try to avoid the job, so it is worth checking that the 'cats' (one in the middle of each exhaust downpipe, at the back of the engine) are present. If the 'cat' rattles at idle when the engine is warm, it probably needs replacing. Needless to say, a vehicle originally fitted with a catalytic converter exhaust is required to have one to meet roadworthiness regulations in most countries.

There have been several aftermarket suppliers of 'sports' exhausts for the Range Rover. Typically, these systems dispense with the centre silencer, so reducing the back pressure and allowing the engine to breathe more freely; an inevitable result (and one that attracts many buyers) is that the exhaust sounds louder and more sporty. There is no particular problem with such exhaust systems, as long as you are happy with the higher level of noise.

While examining the exhaust, it's worth checking the state of the tailpipe, too. On diesel models, the inside of the exhaust pipe is likely to be a black colour. On petrol models, a light grey deposit inside the pipe is a good sign, but a powdery black deposit suggests the engine is running rich or that the vehicle has been used excessively in low-speed town traffic.

When the engine is running, steam from the exhaust of either a petrol or diesel engine suggests head gasket problems (although there may be a small amount on starting a cold engine, caused by condensation in the exhaust pipe). White smoke may point to a leak from the brake servo.

Electrical system

The electrical system is the Range Rover's Achilles heel. It was far more complex than any that Land Rover had used on a vehicle before, and was far from perfect when the vehicle was launched. It did improve over the years, however, and Range Rovers built after about 1998 are much less prone to problems. However, some bizarre problems can be caused by something as simple as a poor earth contact, and, longer term, it is as well to buy a workshop manual and find out where the main earthing points are located.

Central to many electrical functions is the Body Electronic Control Module (BECM), which monitors signals from various electrical systems around the vehicle. One of its functions is to prevent problems caused by potentially conflicting demands on the electrical system (so, for example, it will prevent the air suspension from changing height when a door is open). However, this interdependence of

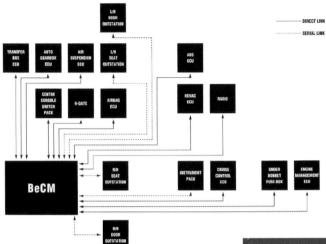

DIRECT LINK
SERIAL LINK

TRANSFER BOX ECU

AUTO GEARBOX ECU

AIR SUSPENSION ECU

L/H SEAT OUTSTATION

L/H DOOR OUTSTATION

CENTRE CONSOLE SWITCH PACK

H-GATE

AIRBAG ECU

HEVAC ECU

RADIO

ABS ECU

BeCM

R/H SEAT OUTSTATION

INSTRUMENT PACK

CRUISE CONTROL ECU

UNDER BONNET FUSE BOX

ENGINE MANAGEMENT ECU

R/H DOOR OUTSTATION

If you need any persuading that the BeCM is best left alone, take a look at this schematic diagram which shows how it is connected to multiple other onboard systems!

systems can also make it hard to trace the cause of some faults.

Also worth knowing is that there are several Electronic Control Units (ECUs) underneath the right-hand front seat. This makes them reasonably accessible but it also makes them vulnerable to water damage, either from leaks or from a faulty door seal when the vehicle is waded. A visual check for corrosion around the terminals is a good idea.

The best general advice is to make sure that everything electrical works on the vehicle you are looking at. Lights are a bare minimum for legal and safety reasons, but take a long and careful look at any wiring that wasn't original to the vehicle, and be deeply suspicious of wires that seem to go nowhere! Remember, too, that it's not unknown for additional equipment to overload the original wiring and burn it out.

Start by checking that all the electric windows work properly (yes, you did this on your earlier check, but do it again), and check the operation of the sunroof as well. It's a tilt-and-slide type, so make sure it does all the

The function of every switch needs to be checked. These are the ones for the air suspension system.

The sunroof is a tilt-and-slide type, and it needs to work properly!

things it's supposed to do. Check the central locking, the electric seat adjustment and front seat heaters (when fitted), and even the ICE system. Some late models have screens for a satellite navigation system, and you need to make sure that this works. These systems require an annual subscription (and a new disc) if they are to be updated with all the latest information, and it is highly unlikely that the owner

This picture gives a good idea of the multiple switches that need to be tested – and this Range Rover has the less complicated 'standard' heating system.

More switches: these are the controls for the automatic climate control system fitted to better-equipped models. The digital readout allows the desired temperature for each side of the car to be set, and the system then endeavours to achieve it.

Check the correct functioning of the CD stacker in the rear, if one is fitted.

of an elderly Range Rover will have bothered with the expense; the system may still work, but it will not be fully up to date.

Finally, it is worth knowing that many of the major electrical components (especially the ECUs) are 'synchronised' to the vehicle: that is, they are electronically embedded with the vehicle's VIN and will not work if transferred to another vehicle. This is a wonderful anti-theft system, but it does mean that you can't replace such components with secondhand ones from another vehicle!

Convenience features

The second-generation Range Rover majored on convenience features, which were essential for it to compete with conventional saloons in the luxury class. Most of these are electrically operated (see the section above), but many of them are best checked from the driving seat. Now is the time to check everything operated by a switch or a button that you have not already checked. It will be a rare and well cared for vehicle that does not throw up at least one fault!

Look for missing pixels on the LCD dashboard displays: a common fault usually caused by poor contact between the ribbon cable and the LCD display. There is a DIY fix for this, and a new ribbon cable is not expensive, but the job is tricky and time-consuming – so a fault here is definitely worth using as a bargaining point!

The next thing to test is the HEVAC system – the Range Rover's complex Heating, Ventilation and Air-conditioning system. All models except the early entry-level types have automatic temperature control, which depends on sensors inside the vehicle that report cabin temperature to its control ECU. The ECU then instructs a series of servo-operated flaps, and the blower fans, to put more heat into the cabin or to turn on the air-conditioning, as appropriate to reach the target temperature set on the control panel. The air-conditioning can be switched off altogether (to save the extra fuel used as the engine drives the compressor), when a warning light should illuminate on the control panel.

There is a useful set of checks that will help you discover whether everything is working as it should, but you should only carry them out with the engine running, as they are quite demanding of battery power. Begin by hitting the 'Prog' button (the name is short for Programmed Defrost). This should automatically direct warm air to the windscreen, increase the fan speed, and switch on the heated rear window and heated windscreen. Hit the button again to turn the system off (the heated screens may remain on), and turn the temperature on each side of the vehicle down to its minimum setting. This should automatically engage the air-conditioning system, even if it has been set to 'off,' and the fans, and begin to produce refrigerated air.

On older or neglected Range Rovers, the fan motors may have stopped working, or may be working at reduced speed. Replacing them is an involved and time-consuming job, and is not to be recommended to anyone with only average or lower DIY skills. So a fault here should be another bargaining point. Poor blower performance may be caused by clogged pollen filters, as the HEVAC system draws in air through these. There are two of them, one at each end of the bulkhead underneath a plastic cover just below the windscreen, and they are cheap and easy to replace. Ask when they were last changed; you may well find that the seller didn't know there were any!

If there is no heat at all from the heater on a diesel-engined Range Rover, the problem almost certainly lies with a failing water pump. You will want to get this changed as quickly as possible because it will lead to overheating of the engine. It is not an expensive part, and a problem here may well lead you to question why the seller has not already attended to it.

There is one more problem associated with the HEVAC system, and that is leaks from the heater. Your checks for dampness in the footwells should have revealed whether this problem is present, and it is very likely to be caused by hardening of the rubber O-rings between the heater itself and the aluminium heater pipes from the engine. Replacement requires some major dismantling, for which Land Rover used to allocate 12 hours of workshop time. There are quicker ways to do the job (and you can find them on the internet), but this is another problem that can be used to negotiate the asking price of the vehicle.

Test drive

You will want to take the vehicle for a proper test drive before making your mind up whether to buy it. Double-check the position on insurance, and that the vehicle remains road legal; both insurance and roadworthiness certificate may have expired since your previous look.

Engine health and performance   4️⃣   3️⃣   2️⃣   1️⃣

Most people assume the health of the engine is the first thing to check on a test drive. So we'll start with that, but remember that it isn't always the engine that causes the most expensive problems!

(a) The BMW diesel The six-cylinder diesel should pull quite smoothly through the gears, and should not feel sluggish at low speeds. It is far better suited to a manual gearbox, and many people find the combination of diesel engine and automatic gearbox unpalatable.

Keep an eye on the engine temperature gauge, because these engines can overheat, which may lead to expensive problems such as a cracked cylinder head. If there is a strong smell of hot coolant after the engine has been running for a while, try to discover where it is coming from.

When you return from your test drive, allow the warm engine to idle for a few seconds. Then blip the accelerator and check in the mirror for black smoke from the exhaust. If there is some, the engine is worn.

(b) The petrol V8s Enthusiasts love the petrol V8s for their smooth and refined power delivery, and any engine that falls short of the mark should be treated with suspicion. Listen for top-end noise (the hydraulic tappets can gum up, and the camshaft can wear), and beware of misfires, which are not always easy to detect in a multi-cylinder engine. A rough and rasping sound from one side of the engine usually means that the exhaust manifold is blowing; it's unlikely to be cracked, and the remedy will probably just be to tighten the manifold bolts.

Gearbox assessment

(a) Manual gearbox The manual gearbox is the five-speed R380 type (R for Rover Group, 380 for its torque capacity in Nm). There were some selection problems on early examples of this gearbox, but they were all sorted out under warranty, and gear selection should be smooth and baulk-free.

However, high-mileage gearboxes can suffer from mainshaft wear and synchromesh problems, and sometimes no gear can be engaged until the gearbox has warmed up. Third gear seems to be most affected, so listen for a crunch as it's selected and as you change down to second. The R380 was deliberately designed to give slick, car-like changes, and something is wrong if it doesn't. Check, too, for a worn layshaft, which is betrayed by a rattle in neutral with the engine running.

The five-speed manual gearbox is seen here in a demonstration chassis. Low range in the transfer box is selected by a switch on the dashboard.

Nevertheless, these gearboxes are quite capable of functioning for a very long time despite problems caused by wear. Be gentle with a worn one, and aim to fix it or replace it later. You can use demonstrable wear as a bargaining point.

If the clutch squeals when you push the pedal to the floor, the release bearing is probably worn. The parts are not expensive, but fitting can be costly unless you do it yourself, in which case it will take quite a long time. If vehicle speed doesn't increase when you press the accelerator, the clutch is worn and is slipping. Expect the clutch to bite when the pedal is about halfway through its travel; near the top or near the bottom means the adjustment isn't right. Finally, if there's clutch judder as the drive is taken up, you'll need to take a closer look. Harsh gearchanges may result from a worn clutch fork if there is no fault in the gearbox itself.

(b) Automatic gearbox The ZF four-speed automatic gearboxes are very robust and

The automatic gearbox has an H-gate, and low range is automatically selected when the lever is operated in the left-hand arm of the H. This is a right-hand drive Range Rover: the positions of the high range and low range elements in the selector gate swap sides on left-hand drive models.

reliable. You checked for excessive clunks and jerks as the drive is taken up when you took your first look at this Range Rover: try it again now. On the move, changes are normally not very noticeable, so look out for any hesitation or slurring as the box changes up; it probably means the internal clutches are worn. A further important check is to engage Sport mode; if it refuses to engage, there is a problem with the gearbox ECU.

Transfer gearbox and differential lock

You checked that low ratio engages during your preliminary evaluation. Check it again, just to be sure.

Steering and suspension

The steering on one of these Range Rovers is generally well-weighted and well suited to the vehicle. If the vehicle you're testing suffers from wander, the problem is probably worn ball joints. If there seems to be rear-end steering when cornering, the rear radius arm bushes are probably worn; check by accelerating and then lifting off the pedal when cornering.

If the steering seems graunchy or notchy when you turn the wheel, the cause may be worn joints in the steering column. A low level of PAS oil will have a similar effect (but you did check this earlier, didn't you?), and so will a slipping auxiliary drivebelt that drives the PAS pump.

On the move, you are unlikely to discover any problems with the air suspension that were not apparent when the vehicle was standing still. However, listen carefully for the rumble of worn wheel bearings, which tend to last for about 130,000 miles. The vehicle will remain driveable for some time with worn bearings, but you will need to replace them (or it – there may be only one) sooner or later, so use this knowledge to help you haggle with the vendor.

Brakes and traction control

The standard all-disc braking system with vacuum servo assistance and ABS should pull the vehicle up quickly and in a straight line. Any vibration that feeds back through the pedal will probably be caused by rusty or – worse – warped discs. Land Rover aficionados will already know this, but to anyone new to the marque, do NOT test the handbrake by applying it when the vehicle is moving. The handbrake operates on the transmission and not the wheels, and applying it on the move may cause some expensive damage.

When you turn the ignition on, you will hear a buzzing noise for around five or ten seconds. This is the ABS pump priming the pressure accumulator, and from time to time it will recharge the accumulator and make that buzzing noise again. However, if the noise occurs every time you press the brake pedal, there is an internal leak and the accumulator will need to be replaced. Note that if a loss of grip causes the ABS system to activate, it will pump the brakes rapidly and making a chattering noise, which can be alarming until you recognise what it is.

Land Rover used the ABS system on the Range Rover to operate an Electronic Traction Control (ETC) system as well. This uses the wheel sensors to detect wheel slip and will pulse the brake on the affected wheel until traction is regained. This pulsing is accompanied by the same chattering noise that the ABS makes. On early second-generation Range Rovers, ETC operated only on the rear axle; it was extended to all four wheels (sometimes known as 4ETC) in autumn 1998 for the 1999 models. These models did not feature Hill Descent Control, another system that used the ABS hardware, even though it was available on other Land Rover models after 1997.

Paperwork and last-minute checks

You looked at the paperwork when you did your preliminary assessment. Now's the time to double-check that everything is in order, and bear in mind that to fully understand the vehicle, you really do need the driver's handbook that was supplied with it when new. If it isn't present, use the fact to help haggle the price down a bit – and then go and find a handbook on the internet or at an autojumble.

You should also make sure that there are two keys with the vehicle. You only need one to drive it, but you need a spare in case you lose that, or to suit a second driver. These keys are expensive because they incorporate a

You checked the interior before, but check again. A close look shows that the cigarette lighter is missing here.

If you haven't already looked under the boot floor, it's important to do it as one of the last-minute checks. Is there a spare wheel? Are the wheel-changing tools all present?

The key fob incorporates buttons for the remote central locking, and the shaft of the key itself folds away into the fob. You need two keys: they are expensive!

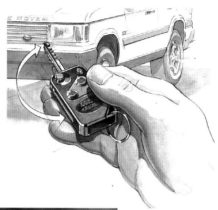

transponder that is part of the anti-theft system, they can only be obtained through Land Rover dealerships, and they must be programmed ('synchronised') to suit the individual vehicle. Buying a secondhand key is simply not an option, because the keys cannot be reprogrammed to suit a second vehicle.

Only a road test will show you whether the Range Rover rides and drives as serenely as it should. This one is a late Vogue SE model.

Evaluation procedure

Add up the total points, and see what category the vehicle falls into. The maximum possible score is 100.

85 points = Excellent
70 points = Good
55 points = Average
40 points = Poor

A Range Rover scoring over 70 will be completely usable and will need only regular care and maintenance to preserve its condition. A score between 50 and 60 means some work is needed, and this is likely to cost about the same regardless of the actual score. A score lower than 50 means that you are looking at some major restoration work, in which case it may be preferable to buy a better vehicle.

10 Auctions

– sold! Another way to buy your dream

Auction pros & cons

Pros: Prices will usually be lower than those of dealers or private sellers and you might grab a real bargain on the day. Auctioneers have usually established clear title with the seller. At the venue you can usually examine documentation relating to the vehicle.

Cons: You have to rely on a sketchy catalogue description of condition and history. The opportunity to inspect is limited, and you cannot drive the car. Auction cars are often a little below par and may require some work. It's easy to overbid. There will usually be a buyer's premium to pay in addition to the auction hammer price.

Which auction?

Auctions by established auctioneers are advertised in car magazines and on the auction houses' websites. A catalogue, or a simple printed list of the lots for auctions might only be available a day or two ahead, though often lots are listed and pictured on auctioneers' websites much earlier. Contact the auction company to ask if previous auction selling prices are available as this is useful information (details of past sales are often available on websites).

Catalogue, entry fee and payment details

When you purchase the catalogue of the vehicles in the auction, it often acts as a ticket allowing two people to attend the viewing days and the auction. Catalogue details tend to be comparatively brief, but will include information such as 'one owner from new, low mileage, full service history,' etc. It will also usually show a guide price to give you some idea of what to expect to pay and will tell you what is charged as a 'Buyer's premium.' The catalogue will also contain details of acceptable forms of payment. At the fall of the hammer an immediate deposit is usually required, the balance payable within 24 hours. If the plan is to pay by cash there may be a cash limit. Some auctions will accept payment by debit card. Sometimes credit or charge cards are acceptable, but will often incur an extra charge. A bank draft or bank transfer will have to be arranged in advance with your own bank as well as with the auction house. No vehicle will be released before **all** payments are cleared. If delays occur in payment transfers then storage costs can accrue.

Buyer's premium

A buyer's premium will be added to the hammer price: **don't** forget this in your calculations. It is not usual for there to be a further state tax or local tax on the purchase price and/or on the buyer's premium.

Viewing

In some instances it's possible to view on the day, or days before, as well as in the hours prior to, the auction. There are auction officials available who are willing to help out by opening engine and luggage compartments and to allow you to inspect the interior. While the officials may start the engine for you, a test drive is out of the question. Crawling under and around the car as much as you want is permitted, but you can't suggest that the car you are interested in be jacked up, or attempt to do the job yourself. You can also ask to see any documentation available.

Bidding

Before you take part in the auction, **decide your maximum bid – and stick to it!** It may take a while for the auctioneer to reach the lot you are interested in, so use that time to observe how other bidders behave. When it's the turn of your car, attract the auctioneer's attention and make an early bid. The auctioneer will then look to you for a reaction every time another bid is made; usually the bids will be in fixed increments until the bidding slows, when smaller increments will often be accepted before the hammer falls. If you want to withdraw from the bidding, make sure the auctioneer understands your intentions – a vigorous shake of the head when he or she looks to you for the next bid should do the trick!

Assuming that you are the successful bidder, the auctioneer will note your card or paddle number, and from that moment on you will be responsible for the vehicle. If the car is unsold, either because it failed to reach the reserve or because there was little interest, it may be possible to negotiate with the owner, via the auctioneers, after the sale is over.

Successful bid

There are two more items to think about. How to get the vehicle home, and insurance. If you can't drive it, your own or a hired trailer is one way; another is to have the vehicle shipped using the facilities of a local company. The auction house will also have details of companies specialising in the transfer of cars.

Insurance for immediate cover can usually be purchased on site, but it may be more cost-effective to make arrangements with your own insurance company in advance, and then call to confirm the full details.

eBay & other online auctions?

eBay & other online auctions could land you a vehicle at a bargain price, though you'd be foolhardy to bid without examining it first, something most vendors encourage. A useful feature of eBay is that the geographical location of the vehicle is shown, so you can narrow your choices to those within a realistic radius of home. Be prepared to be outbid in the last few moments of the auction. Remember, your bid is binding and that it will be very, very difficult to get restitution in the case of a crooked vendor fleecing you – **caveat emptor!**

Be aware that some vehicles offered for sale in online auctions are 'ghost' cars. **Don't** part with **any** cash without being sure that the vehicle does actually exist and is as described (usually pre-bidding inspection is possible).

Auctioneers

Barrett-Jackson www.barrett-jackson.com/ **Bonhams** www.bonhams.com/ **British Car Auctions BCA)** www.bca-europe.com or www.british-car-auctions. co.uk/ **Cheffins** www.cheffins.co.uk/ **Christies** www.christies.com/ **Coys** www. coys.co.uk/ **eBay** www.ebay.com/ **H&H** www.classic-auctions.co.uk/ **RM** www. rmauctions.com/ **Shannons** www.shannons.com.au/ **Silver** www.silverauctions. com

11 Paperwork
– correct documentation is essential!

The paper trail
Classic, collector and prestige cars usually come with a large portfolio of paperwork accumulated and passed on by a succession of proud owners. This documentation represents the real history of the car and from it can be deduced the level of care the car has received, how much it's been used, which specialists have worked on it and the dates of major repairs and restorations. All of this information will be priceless to you as the new owner, so be very wary of cars with little paperwork to support their claimed history.

Registration documents
All countries/states have some form of registration for private vehicles whether its like the American 'pink slip' system or the British 'log book' system.

It is essential to check that the registration document is genuine, that it relates to the car in question, and that all the vehicle's details are correctly recorded, including chassis/VIN and engine numbers (if these are shown). If you are buying from the previous owner, his or her name and address will be recorded in the document: this will not be the case if you are buying from a dealer.

In the UK the current (Euro-aligned) registration document is named V5C, and is printed in coloured sections of blue, green and pink. The blue section relates to the car specification, the green section has details of the new owner and the pink section is sent to the DVLA in the UK when the car is sold. A small section in yellow deals with selling the car within the motor trade.

In the UK the DVLA will provide details of earlier keepers of the vehicle upon payment of a small fee, and much can be learned in this way.

If the car has a foreign registration there may be expensive and time-consuming formalities to complete. Do you really want the hassle?

Roadworthiness certificate
Most country/state administrations require that vehicles are regularly tested to prove that they are safe to use on the public highway and do not produce excessive emissions. In the UK that test (the 'MoT') is carried out at approved testing stations, for a fee. In the USA the requirement varies, but most states insist on an emissions test every two years as a minimum, while the police are charged with pulling over unsafe-looking vehicles.

In the UK the test is required on an annual basis once a vehicle becomes three years old. Of particular relevance for older cars is that the certificate issued includes the mileage reading recorded at the test date and, therefore, becomes an independent record of that car's history. Ask the seller if previous certificates are available. Without an MoT the vehicle should be trailered to its new home, unless you insist that a valid MoT is part of the deal. (Not such a bad idea this, as at least you will know the car was roadworthy on the day it was tested and you don't need to wait for the old certificate to expire before having the test done.)

Road licence
The administration of every country/state charges some kind of tax for the use of its

To get the most out of a Range Rover, you really do need to ensure that the owner's handbook is among the papers with it. This is an early one, from a 1995 model ...

road system, the actual form of the 'road licence' and, how it is displayed, varying enormously country to country and state to state.

Whatever the form of the 'road licence', it must relate to the vehicle carrying it and must be present and valid if the car is to be driven on the public highway legally. The value of the licence will depend on the length of time it will continue to be valid. In the UK if a car is untaxed because it has not been used for a period of time, the owner has to inform the licencing authorities, otherwise the vehicle's date-related registration number will be lost and there will be a painful amount of paperwork to get it re-registered.

Valuation certificate
Hopefully, the vendor will have a recent valuation certificate, or letter signed by a recognised expert stating how much he, or she, believes the particular car to be worth (such documents, together with photos, are usually needed to get 'agreed value' insurance). Generally such documents should act only as confirmation of your own assessment of the car rather than a guarantee of value as the expert has probably not seen the car in the flesh. The easiest way to find out how to obtain a formal valuation is to contact the owners' club.

Service history
Often these cars will have been serviced at home by enthusiastic (and hopefully capable) owners for a good number of years. Nevertheless, try to obtain as much service history and other paperwork pertaining to the car as you can. Naturally, dealer stamps, or specialist garage receipts score most points in the value stakes. However, anything helps in the great authenticity game, items like the original bill of sale, handbook, parts invoices and repair bills, adding to the story and the character of the car. Even a brochure correct to the year of the car's manufacture is a useful

... and this is the later type, which came in a special pouch. The *Quick Guide to Driving Controls* really is a help if you're new to the model!

document and something that you could well have to search hard to locate in future years. If the seller claims that the car has been restored, then expect receipts and other evidence from a specialist restorer.

If the seller claims to have carried out regular servicing, ask what work was completed, when, and seek some evidence of it being carried out. Your assessment of the car's overall condition should tell you whether the seller's claims are genuine.

Restoration photographs

If the seller tells you that the car has been restored, then expect to be shown a series of photographs taken while the restoration was under way. Pictures taken at various stages, and from various angles, should help you gauge the thoroughness of the work. If you buy the car, ask if you can have all the photographs as they form an important part of the vehicle's history. It's surprising how many sellers are happy to part with their car and accept your cash, but want to hang on to their photographs! In the latter event, you may be able to persuade the vendor to get a set of copies made.

12 What's it worth?

– let your head rule your heart

Condition

If the Range Rover you've been looking at is really bad, then you've probably not bothered to use the marking system in chapter 9 – the 60 minute evaluation. You may not have even got as far as using that chapter at all!

If you did use the marking system in chapter 9 you'll know whether the car is in Excellent (maybe Concours), Good, Average or Poor condition, or, perhaps, somewhere in-between these categories.

Many specialist magazines run a regular price guide. If you haven't bought the latest editions, do so now

The later front end with clear indicator lenses and headlamp 'masks' may be more attractive than the earlier type – but that does not automatically make it worth more.

and compare their suggested values for the model you are thinking of buying: also look at the auction prices they're reporting. Values of second-generation Range Rovers were not high at the time of writing – in fact, good ones could be had at bargain-basement prices – but never forget that trends can change, and sometimes surprisingly quickly.

The values published in the magazines tend to vary from one magazine to another, as do their scales of condition, so read carefully the guidance notes they provide. Bear in mind that a car that is truly a recent show winner could be worth more than the highest scale published. Assuming that the car you have in mind is not in show/concours condition, then relate the level of condition that you judge

the car to be in with the appropriate guide price. How does the figure compare with the asking price? Before you start haggling with the seller, consider what effect any variation from standard specification might have on the car's value.

If you are buying from a dealer, remember there will be a dealer's premium on the price.

Desirable options/extras

Many owners consider the most desirable of these Range Rovers are the later ones with the Thor V8 engines, and of course the higher specification levels of the Vogue

These late 'Comet' wheels were more attractive than earlier designs, but again do not actually add to the intrinsic value of a Range Rover.

Many second-generation Range Rovers were used by police forces as motorway patrol vehicles. Some ex-police vehicles are still around, but they will have high mileage, and there may be various holes and brackets where equipment has been removed. Argue the price down accordingly!

models have a special attraction. Extras are much more a matter of personal preference. For example, side-steps may not improve the appearance of the Range Rover, but they may be necessary for some people just to get into the vehicle, which sits quite high off the ground.

Some people also insist on the best and the biggest of everything, and so nothing less than a 4.6-litre engine will do. The reality is that, in everyday use, the 4.0-litre V8 is just as good; after all, it is not every day that you need to drive your Range Rover at 125mph!

Undesirable features

Generally speaking, non-original features will detract from a vehicle's value – and maybe from its interest as well, if you're looking for a Range Rover that's truly representative of the way they were. There are exceptions, such as the properly engineered high-performance conversions by Overfinch or JE Engineering, but these are rather a specialist interest anyway. Avoid anything with a non-original paint scheme and non-original interior unless it is a documented Autobiography model.

There are many people who would argue that an automatic diesel model is undesirable *per se* because of its poor performance. Perhaps so; but why not try one before making up your mind?

Whether you want aftermarket accessories that were contemporary with the vehicle is a matter of personal choice. Arguably, they were part of the way it was when new or nearly new. Another argument is that they were not fitted by the factory or one of its dealers and are therefore not 'original.'

The Autobiography models generally have extra or unusual features, and rarity persuades sellers to ask higher prices than for standard production models.

Very rare, and almost certainly pricey, is the S500 supercharged conversion from JE Engineering.

The twin-airbag installation was not universal, but any Range Rover for sale in the UK without both airbags will be an import. This one was sold new in South Africa.

Striking a deal

Negotiate on the basis of your condition assessment, mileage, and fault rectification cost. Also take into account the car's specification. Be realistic about the value, but don't be completely intractable: a small compromise on the part of the vendor or buyer will often facilitate a deal at little real cost.

13 Do you really want to restore?

– it'll take longer and cost more than you think

What do you mean by restoration? At the time of writing, complete restorations of second-generation Range Rovers were almost non-existent. One reason was generally low values; another was the model's reputation for being troublesome; and the third was that some parts could not be found in good condition for love or money. It's to be hoped that this position will change in time, but now really is not the time to try restoring a derelict example.

By contrast, a rolling restoration is and probably always will be a realistic proposition. This way of doing things allows the Range Rover to remain useable for most of the time and allows you to improve it in larger or smaller bites as you go along. Ultimately, it's very rewarding because you can see a gradual process of improvement.

Cost will play a very big part in what you do. Sadly, it's well known that any restoration will take twice as long and cost at least twice as much as your original, hard-headed estimate – although that has never deterred a committed enthusiast. Above all, don't run away with the idea that you will be able to sell the completed vehicle for more than

The first production Range Rover still survives in preservation, as an example of the way the earliest models were. However, if it had not been carefully preserved from new, it is doubtful whether even as important an example as this would justify the typical costs of restoration.

The leather upholstery that contributes so much to the appeal of this interior (the model has an SE specification) is very expensive to replace once it has become worn and damaged.

you have spent on it. Prices might rise eventually, but not soon enough for you to care.

So if you decide to restore a Range Rover, restore it for yourself. Restore it to your standards, to your time-scale, and to your budget. Even if you have the skills, the equipment and the premises to do the job, resign yourself to having no free weekends for at least a couple of years. If you don't have all these vital elements and are paying somebody else to do the work, resign yourself to having no money to spend on anything else for a similar period of time: classic car restorers can and do charge handsomely for deploying their skills. And whichever way you decide

Mechanical restoration is in many respects the easiest part! This is the Thor V8 engine under the bonnet of a late model Range Rover.

to go, resign yourself to frustrating waits while vital parts are sourced – or, in a worst case, remade from scratch.

If all this sounds like a counsel of despair, it really isn't. If you are really committed to getting that Range Rover up and running and looking the way you think it should, the time, the effort and the money will all be worth it in the end. There is nothing quite like the first test drive in your newly-restored Range Rover, even if it does break down after the first 100 yards because you've forgotten to tighten something vital. And after that, every little improvement you make will make you feel prouder and prouder. It may well become a lifetime's commitment, but you will probably find that it's worth it. To you, at least.

Superb when properly maintained and fully functioning, but an expensive nightmare when not – this is the cabin of a late US-spec model.

14 Paint problems
– bad complexion, including dimples, pimples and bubbles

Paint faults generally occur due lack of protection/maintenance, or to poor preparation prior to a respray or touch-up. Some of the following conditions may be present in the car you're looking at:

Orange peel
This appears as an uneven paint surface, similar to the appearance of the skin of an orange. The fault is caused by the failure of atomized paint droplets to flow into each other when they hit the surface. It's sometimes possible to rub out the effect with proprietary paint cutting/rubbing compound or very fine grades of abrasive paper. A respray may be necessary in severe cases. Consult a bodywork repairer/paint shop for advice on the particular car.

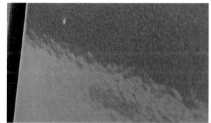

Cracking
Severe cases are likely to have been caused by too heavy an application of paint (or filler beneath the paint). Also, insufficient stirring of the paint before application can lead to the components being improperly mixed, and cracking can result. Incompatibility with the paint already on the panel can have a similar effect. To rectify the problem it is necessary to rub down to a smooth, sound finish before respraying the problem area.

Crazing
Sometimes the paint takes on a crazed rather than a cracked appearance when the problems mentioned under 'Cracking' are present. This problem can also be caused by a reaction between the underlying surface and the paint. Paint removal and respraying the problem area is usually the only solution.

Blistering
Almost always caused by corrosion of the metal beneath the paint. Perforation is likely to be found in the metal, and the damage will usually be worse than that

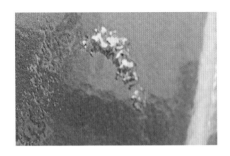 

suggested by the area of blistering. The metal will have to be repaired before repainting.

Micro blistering

Usually the result of an economy respray where inadequate heating has allowed moisture to settle on the car before spraying. Consult a paint specialist, but usually damaged paint will have to be removed before partial or full respraying. Can also be caused by car covers that don't 'breathe.'

Fading

Some colours, especially reds, are prone to fading if subjected to strong sunlight for long periods without the benefit of polish protection. Sometimes proprietary paint restorers and/or paint cutting/rubbing compounds will retrieve the situation. Often a respray is the only real solution.

Peeling

Often a problem with metallic paintwork is when the sealing lacquer becomes damaged and begins to peel off. Poorly applied paint may also peel. The remedy is to strip and start again!

Dimples

Dimples in the paintwork are caused by the residue of polish (particularly silicone types) not being removed properly before respraying. Paint removal and repainting is the only solution.

Dents

Small dents are usually easily cured by the 'Dentmaster,' or equivalent process, that sucks or pushes out the dent (as long as the paint surface is still intact). Companies offering dent removal services usually come to your home: consult your telephone directory.

15 Problems due to lack of use
– just like their owners, Range Rovers need exercise!

Cars, like humans, are at their most efficient if they exercise regularly. A run of at least ten miles, once a week, is recommended for classics.

Seized components
Pistons in calipers, slave and master cylinders can seize. The clutch may seize if the plate becomes stuck to the flywheel because of corrosion. Handbrakes (parking brakes) can seize if the cables and linkages rust. Pistons can seize in the bores due to corrosion.

Fluids
Old, acidic oil can corrode bearings. Uninhibited coolant can corrode internal waterways – a particular problem with the V8 engine, which has aluminium heads and block. Lack of antifreeze can cause core plugs to be pushed out; even cracks in the block or head. Silt settling and solidifying can cause overheating.

Brake fluid absorbs water from the atmosphere, and should be renewed every two years. Old fluid with a high water content can cause corrosion and pistons/

Out of use for many years, this Range Rover will need a lot of money spent on it to restore it to as-new condition.

calipers to seize (freeze) and can cause brake failure when the water turns to vapour near hot braking components.

Tyre problems
Tyres that have had the weight of the car on them in a single position for some time will develop flat spots, resulting in some (usually temporary) vibration. The tyre walls may have cracks or (blister-type) bulges, meaning new tyres are needed.

Shock absorbers (dampers)
With lack of use, the dampers will lose their elasticity or even seize. Creaking, groaning and stiff suspension are signs of this problem.

Rubber and plastic
Radiator hoses may have perished and split, possibly resulting in the loss of all coolant. Window and door seals can harden and leak. Gaiters/boots can crack. Wiper blades will harden.

Electrics
The battery will be of little use if it has not been charged for many months, and a flat battery can cause all sorts of electrical problems in one of these Range Rovers.

Earthing/grounding problems are common when the connections have corroded. The Range Rover's electrics depend heavily on shaped plastic block connectors, and unless there's a specific problem, it's wise to leave these undisturbed. Sparkplug electrodes will often have corroded in an unused engine. Wiring insulation, especially in the engine bay, can harden and fail.

Rotting exhaust system
Exhaust gas contains a high water content so exhaust systems corrode very quickly from the inside when the vehicle is not used.

Air suspension
All models of second-generation Range Rover were originally built with air suspension, and you should expect to replace the air springs as an absolute minimum on any example that has spent a long time out of use. Height sensors, the compressor, and air reservoir may all need to be replaced as well, before the system will work properly.

16 The Community

– key people, organisations and companies in the Range Rover world

Like Land Rovers, Range Rovers have an enthusiast following that is pretty much worldwide. But from the outset, it is worth remembering that the second-generation Range Rover's problems have been so well known and for so long that you may well have to put up with some good-natured ribbing from fellow enthusiasts about your new vehicle!

There is just not enough space here to cover the key members of the Range Rover community in every country, so these listings are confined to the UK – and even then are far from exhaustive. For details of clubs, specialists and suppliers in other countries, please consult your regional 4x4 or Land Rover magazine, or check on the internet.

There is a reverential interest in important examples of the second-generation Range Rover, and this one is the oldest known survivor. It is a pre-production model, preserved by the Dunsfold Land Rover Trust, and is seen here at one of their displays.

Clubs

There are many local and regional Land Rover clubs in the UK that welcome Range Rovers. However, you may find that the emphasis of your local club is more on off-road driving (typically greenlaning) or on competitive motorsport (typically trialling) than on meticulous restoration for what US enthusiasts call 'show'n'shine' events. Many clubs of course cater for all forms of the hobby.

There is one club that is dedicated to Range Rovers, and covers Range Rovers of all types (not just the second-generation models). This is the Range Rover Register,

By contrast, some owners prefer to customise their vehicles. This example was pictured at an enthusiasts' event, where it won a prize.

The off-road capability of these Range Rovers is immense, and this one has clearly been enjoyed on the Land Rover tracks at Eastnor Castle in Herefordshire. It has been raised to the highest available suspension setting to give maximum ground clearance over tricky obstacles.

which can be found on the web at **www.rrr.co.uk** and can be contacted by telephone on 01908 667901.

Main spares suppliers
John Craddock Ltd, North Street, Bridgtown, Cannock, Staffordshire WS11 0AZ. 01543 577207, or www.johncraddockltd.co.uk
Dunsfold DLR, Alfold Road, Dunsfold, Surrey GU8 4NP. 01483 200567, www.dunsfold.com or
dlr@dunsfold.com
Paddock Spares and Accessories, The Showground, The Cliff, Matlock, Derbyshire DE4 5EW. 01629 760877, www.paddockspares.com or sales@paddockspares.com
Rimmer Brothers, Triumph House, Sleaford Road, Bracebridge Heath, Lincoln LN4 2NA. 01522 568000, www.rimmerbros.co.uk or LRsales@rimmerbros.co.uk

Specialist restorers
Kingsley Cars Ltd, A40 Eynsham Bypass, Eynsham. Witney OX29 4EF. 01865 884488, or sales@kinglseycars.co.uk
Twenty-Ten Engineering, 101 Bartleet Road, Redditch, Worcestershire B98 0DQ. 07973 831878, or enquiries@twentytenengineering.co.uk

Vehicle Information
If you are keen to find out about the history of your own vehicle, start with the archives section of the British Motor Museum at Gaydon (01926 641188). They can normally

Off-road driving is not all about heroics and extremes, despite what the popular press might have you believe. This is a convoy drive through snow in Scotland, organised by the Land Rover Experience and featuring several different vehicles built by the company.

tell you when your Range Rover left the assembly lines, when it left the factory en route for a Land Rover dealer, and who that dealer was. Their records will also reveal what colour it was originally. For a fee, they will provide you with a certificate that contains the available details, and is a worthwhile addition to any enthusiast's vehicle paperwork.

Magazines
Land Rover Monthly, The Publishing House, 2 Brickfields Business Park, Woolpit, Suffolk IP30 9QS. www.lrm.co.uk
Land Rover Owner International, Bauer, Media House, Lynchwood, Peterborough PE2 6EA. www.lro.com

Books
Range Rover, Second Generation, by James Taylor, The Crowood Press Ltd, ISBN 978-1-78500-473-5
Range Rover Takes on the Competition (Brooklands Books Road Test Series) by RM Clarke, Brooklands Books Ltd, ISBN 1-855-20-505-X
Range Rover 4x4 Performance Portfolio, 1995-2001 (Brooklands Books Road Test Series) by RM Clarke, Brooklands Books Ltd, ISBN 1-855-20619-6

17 Vital statistics
– essential data at your fingertips

Production history

It helps to understand what you're looking at if you have some idea of how the second-generation Range Rover evolved during seven years in production. So here's a breakdown of the key changes; there were many more minor ones.

1994	(September) Introduced, with 134bhp 2.5-litre BMW turbocharged diesel, 190bhp 4.0-litre V8 petrol, or 225bhp 4.6-litre V8 petrol engine; manual gearboxes available on diesel and 4.0, automatic gearbox available on 4.0 and 4.6 models; base, SE (DSE) and HSE (4.6 only) trim levels
1995	(September) Automatic diesel models introduced.
1996	(October) Twin-outlet exhausts fitted across the range; diesel engine re-rated to 136bhp
1997	(Summer) First deliveries of custom-finished Autobiography Range Rovers
1998	(September) Revised 'Thor' V8 engines: 185bhp 4.0 and 218bhp 4.6, both with increased torque
1999	(October) Face-lift with masked headlamps, smoked tail light lenses, etc; new top Vogue trim level announced
2002	(February) Last second-generation Range Rover built

Chassis numbers

All second-generation Range Rover models had VIN-type chassis numbers consisting of 17 digits. The last six digits were the serial number, while the first 11 contain information about the specification, as detailed on the next page. Note that there were differences between the 'RoW' (Rest of World) codes and the 'NAS' (North American Specification) codes.

The VIN of a Range Rover will be found on this tamper-proof sticker attached to the bonnet lock platform. This one is SALLPAMW3WA382930, which decodes as a 1998-model diesel automatic with right-hand drive.

The RoW codes break down like this:

SAL Manufacturer code (Rover Group)
LP Range Rover second generation
A Standard (108-inch) wheelbase
M Four-door body
J 4.6-litre V8 petrol engine
   M = 4.0-litre V8 petrol engine
   W = 2.5-litre six-cylinder diesel engine
3 RHD with automatic gearbox
   4 = LHD, automatic
   7 = RHD with 5-speed manual gearbox
   8 = LHD with 5-speed manual gearbox
M Model-year 1995
   T = 1996   **Y** = 2000
   V = 1997   **1** = 2001
   W = 1998   **2** = 2002
   X = 1999
A Assembled at Solihull

The VIN will also be found more
visibly in a small panel visible
through the base of the windscreen
glass. Needless to say, the two
numbers should be the same, and
should tie up with the information on
the vehicle's identity document!

The NAS (North American Specification) prefix codes differed, as follows:

SAL Manufacturer code (Land Rover)
P Range Rover 38A
A Class E, with GEMS engine management
   C = Class E, with Callaway engine
   E = Class E, to Californian specification
   F = Class E, 2000MY, to LEV standards
   L = Class E, feature spec 1
   M = Class E, feature spec 2
   V = Class E, with Bosch engine management
1 Four-door body
2 4.0-litre V8 petrol engine
   4 = 4.6-litre V8 petrol engine
   5 = 4.0-litre V8 to LEV standards
   6 = 4.6-litre V8 to LEV or ULEV standards
   9 = 4.6-litre V8
4 LHD with 4-speed automatic gearbox
1 Security check digit
   (0 to 9, or X)
S Model-year 1995
   T = 1996   **X** = 1999
   V = 1997   **Y** = 2000
   W = 1998   **1** = 2001
A Assembled at Solihull

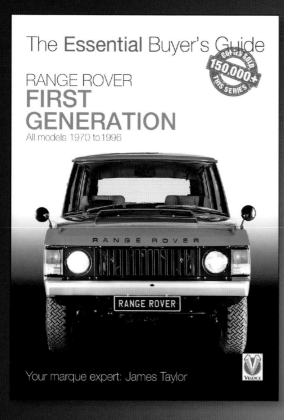

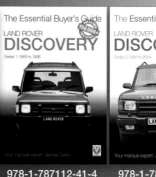

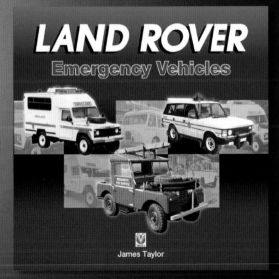

The Essential Buyer's Guide™ series ...

Index